PSALMS 91:

A PRAYER
OF PROTECTION

By Chanell Watkins

Copyright © 2020 by Chanell Watkins

Paperback ISBN: 978-1-7348592-3-2

eBook ISBN: 978-1-73-48592-2-5

All rights reserved. No part of this book may be reproduced or used in any manner without written permission of the copyright owner except for the use of quotations in a book review.

Scriptures marked KJV are taken from the KING JAMES VERSION (KJV): KING JAMES VERSION, public domain.

Published by The Write Legacy LLC

www.thewritelegacy.com

Printed in the United States of America

THE WRITE
LEGACY

Table of Contents

Dedication

Introduction

Psalms 91:1

Psalms 91:2

Psalms 91:3

Psalms 91:4

Psalms 91:5

Psalms 91:6

Psalms 91:7

Psalms 91:8

Psalms 91:9

Psalms 91:10

Psalms 91:11

Psalms 91:12

Psalms 91:13

Psalms 91:14

Psalms 91:15

Psalms 91:16

Meditation Scriptures

Dedication

I would like to dedicate this book to both my spiritual and natural family. You are all so precious to me! Each one of you, name by name, have contributed to the release of this book in more ways than you know! God truly blessed me with His best when it comes to family and for that I am grateful!

Introduction

Prayer is the believer's most powerful gift given to effect change in the heavens and the Earth. It is through prayer and meditation on the Word that we are promised great success and perfect peace. It is by prayer that we communicate with our Father in Heaven and establish His will in the Earth. Today, as believers we often lose hope in prayer because we fail to see the Word manifest in our lives. Our failure first lies in the struggle to plant the Word in our hearts through revelation. Lack of revelation in the heart leaves us with evil hearts of unbelief, unstable in all our ways and unable to receive anything from God. Secondly, we struggle to see the Word in action and mimic (perform) that in our lives. This lack of application limits us to being "hearers" only and not "doers" of the Word.

With the inability to be "doers" of the Word, we are left with what Apostle James calls "dead faith." Dead faith robs us of possessing the promises of God and leaves our prayer life burdened and fruitless.

Praying the Word with Revelation: "Understanding"

To reignite our prayer lives and see the manifestation of the Word of God, there are some basic principles we must first understand.

1. Prayer must be full of the Word of God.

    We are called to establish God's will on the Earth. God's Word is His will. So, prayer must start with the Word and develop from there. The power to create is activated as we pray the Word of God.

2. The Word of God is our new belief system.

When we pray the Word, we must be fully convinced in our heart that it will come to pass. I have found that the most effective way to get the Word in the heart is to confess it repeatedly. Speak it out loud until the Holy Spirit begins to give you revelation and you are fully able to imagine it in your mind. As you meditate on the revelation, your brain is processing it as your reality. In that moment, your brain is being restructured and your heart (mind, will, emotions) is being transformed (reshaped) to the image (mind, will, emotion) of the Son (the Word). Remember, "as a man thinketh in his heart, so is he." -Proverbs 23:7

3. The Word must be continually built up within you.

We must seek a deeper understanding of the Word by letting the Holy Spirit broaden our revelation.

We do this when we meditate on additional Scriptures that reinforce, expand and strengthen the revelation already planted in our heart.

Praying the Word with Revelation: "How-To"

Now that we understand our basic beliefs regarding prayer and the Word, we must now discuss the step-by-step process of "how-to" put these principles into action each time we pray.

1. Begin prayer with Scripture; remind God of His Word (promises).

    Ex: "God, You said in 2 Peter 1:3 that "divine power has given unto us all things that pertain to life and godliness."

2. Confess the Word aloud and make it personal.

Ex: God, You said in 2 Peter 1:3 that "divine power has given unto us all things that pertain to life and godliness," so I declare and decree, "I have everything that I need that pertains to my life and godliness."

3. Ask the Holy Spirit for help.

As you repeatedly confess the Word, it is important that you invite the Holy Spirit in. He is your helper. Ask the Holy Spirit to give you deeper revelation and to paint a picture of how to put the Word into action. Allow Him to give you revelation of how you can apply your declaration (truth, Word) to every area of your life.

4. Declare and decree Your new revelation.

As the Holy Spirit responds to your request for help, begin to declare and decree (pray) the revelation that you receive or the picture that you see. Flow with the Holy Spirit, praying what He reveals, until He stops!

5. Write it down.

Keep a journal of that which the Holy Spirit reveals so that you can continue to declare and decree it until you see it manifest in the Earth (your life). Remember to remain fully convinced, no matter what it may look like, that what you have prayed has already been answered and established in heaven. You are now merely standing in expectation of the moment God releases your requests to the Earth.

6. Go deeper.

Seek more revelation and continue to add to your understanding by finding related Scriptures that help strengthen and expand the Word (revelation) that has been planted in your heart. With new scripture, ask the Holy Spirit for new revelation and a greater vision! Let your new revelation sustain your faith and hope in that which you are expecting.

The intentions of this book: "An Example"

This book uses verse-by-verse revelation of one of the Bible's most well-known Psalms to demonstrate the previously discussed principles and steps. It outlines the process of how we use this knowledge to transition from being a "hearer" only to being a "hearer and doer" well able to see the Word manifest in our lives.

Through this book, the reader is taken on a journey designed to plant an image in their mind that helps them see the Psalm in action. The goal of seeing the Psalm in action is to cause faith (belief) to rise up in their heart (soul) as they come into the understanding of what the promises of the Psalm truly mean and how to apply them to their life.

Arming the reader with faith in the heart and a vision (hope) in their mind, this book goes on to demonstrate how deeper revelation is the birthing place of effectual and fervent prayers! It is in this place of revelation, faith, and prayer that God is able to release unto the believer the grace to manifest and possess that which is now known and understood in the heart!

I pray that as you read this book, fire, power, and zeal will return to your prayer life. I pray that you will encounter God and the manifestation of His Word in a new way. I pray that as you learn effectual and fervent prayer through revelation that God will indeed take you from faith to faith and glory to glory. May every promise prayed be done unto you as you believe, in Jesus' name, Amen!

Now, join me as the Holy Spirit helps me explore through revelation and declare through prayer, Psalms 91: A Prayer of Protection

Psalms 91:1

He that dwelleth in the secret place of the most High shall abide under the shadow of the Almighty.

Confession: I dwell (stay, hide) in the secret (safe) place of the Most High (God). I abide (stay without getting lost) under the shadow (surrounding hedge) of the Almighty (God).

Revelation and Prayer: My secret place (dwelling place) is found in obedience to the Word of God (living the life of Christ). I am safe from the evil one (satisfying the flesh) as I abide in the actions (behavior) and mindset of Jesus Christ (the Word). I continually obey God's will (Word), think with the mind of Christ (the Word) and speak from the heart (Spirit) of God. I remain within the boundaries (obedience) of His commandments (Word), and I am protected. These boundaries keep me hidden in the shadow (finished work, victory) of Christ. This shadow (finished work) is the righteous path that ensures that I abide under the protecting hand of God Almighty. I abide there in full assurance (trust) that I am safe (delivered).

Meditation: Philippians 2:5-8, 3:9; John 14:6; Psalms 5:8

Reflection

Psalms 91:2

I will say of the Lord, He is my refuge and my fortress: my God; in him will I trust.

Confession: The Lord is my refuge (resting place, safety) and my fortress (protection): I am hidden inside Him, and I trust His protection.

Revelation and Prayer: My Lord (ruler) is Jesus Christ (the Word of God). I dwell under (in obedience to) the Word, and the strong presence of God is established around and within me. In this place, my soul is safe (finds refuge) from the harassment (lying thoughts) of the enemy; it is my guard (fortress, strong barrier) against his influence (desires the flesh). His presence (the Word) is my fortress (protection) and is fortified (secure) around me the more I understand, believe and agree with (obey) His decrees (the Word). His presence is a fortress (protection) to every area of my life because His Word (Jesus) has established His government (authority, reign) there. My soul rests here because I trust (firmly believe) in the power (ability) of the Word to be my refuge (defense).

Meditation: John 6:63, Hebrews 4:12, Isaiah 59:19, Exodus 14:14

Reflection

Psalms 91:3

Surely he will deliver thee from the snare of the fowler, and from the noisome pestilence.

Confession: My God (the Word, Truth) delivers me from the snare (entanglement) of the fowler (the enemy), and from the noisome (abusive, harassing) pestilence (disease afflicting the community).

Revelation and Prayer: The Word of God (Jesus, Truth) is the only power that has already and continues to overcome the enemy (lying thoughts). Jesus' (the Word) victory over the enemy (lies) is my assurance that the gates of hell (sin, affliction) cannot prevail (win) against me because the Word (victory) dwells in me. The Word wages war against the knowledge (will, desires) of the enemy that exalts itself against the knowledge (will, desires) of God concerning me. The Word (Truth) disentangles (frees, releases) my trapped soul from the harassing lies (bondage) of the enemy; God predestined me to be conformed (molded, shaped) completely (mind, will and emotion) into the image (God-given vision) of Christ (the Word). I obey His decrees (the Word, Jesus), and they restore life and godliness

(righteousness) to my soul. The Word (Jesus) delivers me from bondage (lies of the enemy) in every area that I am entangled (molded, conformed) with lies and reconfigures (re-shapes) me to the image of Truth (Jesus, the original intent).

Meditation: John 8:43-44, Ephesians 1:4-5, 2 Corinthians 10:4-5, John 15:3, 1 Corinthians 1:3

Reflection

Psalms 91:4

He shall cover thee with his feathers, and under his wings shalt thou trust; His truth shall be thy shield and buckler.

Confession: My Lord (Jesus, the Word) covers (hides) me with His feathers (Spirit), and under His wings (in His arms) I trust (rest): His Truth (Word) is my shield (defense, protection) and buckler (weapon).

Revelation and Prayer: All my trust is in God being who He says He is and the authority of His Word in Heaven and Earth. When the enemy (lying thought) attacks, my faith (governing thoughts) is steadfast (unwavering) in the Word (Truth). I rest in the presence of God as I trust and obey His instructions (the Word). The Spirit of peace surrounds me as I await the manifestation of the Word in the Earth. His instruction (Word, Truth) is my defense (guard, shield) and my weapon (sword) against the enemy (lying thoughts). I am fully convinced that His instruction (Word) is my navigation through the schemes (strategy) of the enemy; it secures victory (deliverance) for my soul (mind, will, emotions).

Meditation: Philippians 2:9-10, Matthew 28:18, John 14:6, John 16:33, John 8:32

Reflection

Psalms 91:5

Thou shalt not be afraid for the terror by night; nor for the arrow that flieth by day

Confession: I am not afraid of the terror (extreme fear) that comes (attacks) at night (in my disobedience, bad times); nor the arrow (lying thoughts, temptation) that flies (speaks to me) by day (in my submission, good times);

Revelation and Prayer: In good times and in bad, I keep my ear inclined to God (the Word) to receive His instruction and obey. Fear (thoughts of the enemy) does not move me from my place of faith (agreeing with God's thoughts). My faith (governing thoughts) remains steadfast in the Word (thoughts of Christ). In moments of fear and temptation, and in good times and understanding, I expect to hear (receive instruction) God's voice (Word). I lean not to my own understanding, and I do not submit (agree with) to fear (lies of the enemy). I resist the temptation to leave the place of rest and protection found in obedience to the Word (Truth). I remain hidden (obedient) in the Word; my spirit and soul are strengthened in faith (thoughts of Christ), and the presence of God is fortified (expanded, infused) in my life even the more.

Meditation: 2 Timothy 1:7, Proverbs 3:5-6, Proverbs 4:20-22, James 4:7, Psalms 62:2

Reflection

Psalms 91:6

Nor for the pestilence that walketh in darkness; nor for the destruction that wasteth at noon day.

Confession: I am not afraid of the pestilence (disease, sickness, death) that is magnified in the dark times (evil times, difficult times); neither the destruction (great loss) that wastes (spills out, floods) at noonday (good times, mountain top).

Revelation and Prayer: I am not moved from my place of faith (strong belief) when the pestilence (disease, death, lies) threatens to overtake my soul (mind, will, emotion) or physical body. I am not moved when trials (tests of faith) and tribulations (difficulties) come in my well-doing. I am not moved when everything around me falls apart and is destroyed or loss seems to overwhelm me. My faith (governing thoughts) remains in the Word (God's thoughts) and its promises. I am persistent to incline my ear and seek God's wisdom (will). I know that all things (situations) work together for my good (benefit). I know that God's Word cannot return to Him void (not fulfilled) and that He cannot lie. I wait with patience for His plan to be revealed to me, through me and in me.

Meditation: 2 Timothy 2:7, James 1:2-5, Romans 8:28, Jeremiah 17:7-8

Reflection

_____
_____
_____
_____
_____
_____
_____
_____
_____
_____
_____
_____

Psalms 91:7

A thousand shall fall at thy side, and ten thousand at thy right hand; but it shall not come nigh thee.

Confession: A thousand of my enemies (harassing thoughts) fall (destroyed by Truth) at my side and ten thousand at my right hand (by the power of God); they cannot come near (influence, overtake) me.

Revelation and Prayer: I do not fear in battle (tests of faith). I trust that Jesus (the Word) has already secured the victory. I release Jesus (the Word) on the scene, and He fights for me. He wages war against every enemy (lying thought) that operates contrary to God's will (Word, desire) for my life. I remain at rest in His shadow (obedience to His Word) and watch as my enemies (every lie) fall (destroyed, exposed) before me.

Meditation: Psalm 23:4, Isaiah 54:17, Revelation 12:11

Reflection

Psalms 91:8

Only with thine eyes shalt thou behold and see the reward of the wicked.

Confession: I (the righteous one) do not behold (suffer, receive) the reward (consequences) of the wicked (unrighteous, those without faith).

Revelation and Prayer: Faith (firm belief) in Jesus (the Word) is my righteousness. I believe (obey) the Word (Jesus), and it is accounted (credited, added) to me as righteousness. Obedience (submission) to the Word (Jesus) leads me in the path of righteousness. Because the righteousness of Christ (the Word) protects me (makes me righteous), I do not receive the reward (destruction) of the wicked (faithless). I am justified through Christ (the Word);

I have the same righteousness (right standing with God) as Jesus Christ.

Meditation: Hebrews 11:6, Romans 14:23, Ephesians 2:8, Romans 4:3, 2 Corinthians 5:21

Reflection

Psalms 91:9

Because thou hast made the Lord, which is my refuge, even the most high thy habitation;

Confession: The Lord (the Word) is my refuge (safe place). The presence of the Most High (God) is my habitation (where I live);

Revelation and Prayer: Jesus (the Word) is my Lord (governing authority). The Word rules (hovers, watches) over me; it is my protection (refuge, safety) from the enemy (evil, lies) because it is my Truth. Submission (obedience) to the Word (life of Christ) is where I abide (dwell, live). I abide in Jesus (the Word) and Jesus and the Most High (God) are one. To abide in obedience to the life of Christ (the Word) is to abide (dwell) in the presence of God (the Most High). The Word abides (lives) in me (my mind, will, emotions), and I abide (remain submitted) in the Word. This is my hiding place.

Meditation: Romans 10:9, John 10:30, John 15:10

Reflection

Psalms 91:10

There shall no evil befall thee, neither shall any plague come nigh thy dwelling.

Confession: No evil (unrighteousness) befalls (overtakes) me; neither does any plague (sickness, disease) come near the place that I dwell (live).

Revelation and Prayer: I abide in Jesus (the Word) as He abides in the Most High (God). Through Jesus (the Word), I abide in the Most High (God), which is the place of love, goodness, righteousness and Truth. The habitation of Truth (obedience to the Word) keeps me protected from the assaults (lies, evil thoughts) released by the evil one to attempt to dislodge my soul (mind, will, emotions) from the place of rest (faith in the Word). I choose to remain at rest in obedience to the Word (righteousness); I choose to rest in the Most High (glory/goodness of God). This place (rest) is my habitation (where I live); no plaque (unrighteousness, sin/lies, death) can come near (influence, overtake) my soul (mind, will, emotions) in this place.

Meditation: Colossians 1:12, Psalms 4:8, John 15:5, Galatians 5:22-23

Reflection

Psalms 91:11

For he shall give his angels charge over thee, to keep thee in all thy ways.

Confession: God's angels have charge (responsibility) over me. I am kept (protected, directed) in all my ways (actions).

Revelation and Prayer: In times of attack (harassing evil, harassing lies), the angels of the Lord are dispatched (assigned) and given charge (authorization, command) to protect (secure) the Word (will of God) spoken over me. The angels bring instruction (answered prayers) to me from the throne room. These instructions (Word of God) keep (guide, direct) me on the path of righteousness (obedience to the Word). The angels work with the Word (Jesus) to keep me in all my ways (direct me to the ways of Christ). The angels fight with the Word (Jesus) to counteract the lies (word of the enemy) that would try to befall (influence, entangle) my soul (mind, will, emotions) and remove me from the place of righteousness (obedience to the Word, Truth).

Meditation: Hebrews 1:14, Daniel 6:22, Psalms 34:7, Psalms 103:20

Reflection

Psalms 91:12

They shall bear thee up in their hands, lest thou dash thy foot against a stone.

Confession: The angels bear (keep) me up (righteous) in their hands (protection). I do not dash (disrupt) my foot (walk, path) against a stone (lie, snare).

Revelation and Prayer: The angels keep me protected (surrounded) as I await instructions from the throne room. They bear me up (strengthen me) in my weakness (lack of knowledge) with the Word of God that they deliver to me. My soul remains in righteousness (protected) because I stay the course (obedient). The angels ensure that I do not go astray while I wait and that no harm comes near me on the way (path of righteousness). The lies (thoughts of the enemy) do not prevail (win) against me (my soul). I remain in obedience to the Word (instruction) from God and His instructions secure (guarantee) my victory.

Meditation: Hebrews 1:14, Psalms 119:105, Joshua 1:8, 1 Corinthians 15:57

Reflection

Psalms 91:13

Thou shalt tread upon the lion and adder: the young lion and dragon shalt thou trample under feet.

Confession: I tread (crush, defeat) upon the lion (strongholds, deep-rooted lies) and adder (snake of death): the young lion (temptation, lying thoughts) and the dragon (full-grown snake) I trample under feet (gain victory).

Revelation and Prayer: The Word (Truth) instructs me toward the path of victory over sin (thoughts and desires contrary to Truth) in every area of my life. I triumph over the temptation (initial desire), root (underlying reason), and fruit (consequences) of sin (lying thoughts) operating in my life. With the Word (Truth), I cast down (reject) the temptation (initial thought) and dismantle (undo) the strongholds (mindset, collection of lies) warring to bring death and bondage to my soul (mind, will, emotion). The

Word (victory of Jesus) detangles (exposes) my soul from every evil work (lie, bondage) and promises my victory (deliverance).

Meditation: James 1:14-15, 1 Corinthians 10:13, Luke 10:19, Mark 16:18

Reflection

Psalms 91:14

Because he hath set his love upon me, therefore will I deliver him: I will set him on high, because he hath known my name.

Confession: Because my love (strong desire to please, obedience) is set upon (directed toward) Him (God), I am delivered: I am set on high (heavenly places) because I know (have experience with, trust) His name.

Revelation and Prayer: God is the object of my affection (love, desire to please). Because I desire to please Him, I trust (have faith in) and obey Him (His Word), and He delivers me (my soul). I am set free from all fear (lack of faith, unbelief) and delivered from all bondage (entanglement) of the enemy (lying thoughts) by His Word (Truth). He gives great attention to me (the deliverance of my soul) because He created me for His purpose. His thoughts (will, Word) regarding me heals me, delivers me, and prepares me for the expected end predestined (already known) before the beginning of time. His Truth (Word) restores my soul to its true identity in the high (heavenly) places as I continue to learn and experience (gain deeper knowledge) Him.

Meditation: John 8:31-32, Colossians 3:2, Jeremiah 29:11, Ephesians 1:4-5, Ephesians 2:6

Reflection

Psalms 91:15

He shall call upon me, and I will answer him: I will be with him in trouble; I will deliver him, and honour him.

Confession: I call upon my God, and He answers me. He is with me in trouble (lack); He delivers me (my soul) and honors (gives place, weight, influence) me.

Revelation and Prayer: I call on (inquire of, seek) my Lord (the Word) in times of trouble (lack of knowledge), and He answers (instructs) me. I rest in trouble (uncertainty) because He (Jesus, the Word) promised to deliver me (cause me to triumph). I am delivered (increased in Truth) when I seek first (honor, give place to) and obey His Word (instruction). As I honor and obey Him (the Word), I grow in His wisdom (thoughts, image, and likeness), and He bestows (rewards) honor (spiritual influence, authority) upon me.

Meditation: Matthew 6:33, Psalms 107:20, 1 Peter 5:6-7, 1 Samuel 2:30

Reflection

Psalms 91:16

With long life will I satisfy him, and shew him my Salvation.

Confession: He satisfies (rewards) me with a long (eternal) life and His salvation (deliverance, peace).

Revelation and Prayer: I obey His Word (life of Jesus), trust His love (desire to do good) and rest in His presence (glory, goodness). In this place of righteousness (faith, trust in Jesus), I am protected from the influence of the enemy (evil thoughts, desires), and salvation (deliverance, revelation of Truth) is bestowed upon my soul (mind, will, emotions). In this secret place (obedience to the Word), I am made whole. I fulfill God's will (original intent) for my life. The reward (satisfaction, completion) of my obedience is the fulfilled hope of eternal life.

Chanell Watkins

Meditation: John 3:16, Romans 5:1, 1 John 5:2

Reflection

Meditation Scriptures

Psalms 91:1

Philippians 2:5-8

Let this mind be in you, which was also in Christ Jesus: Who, being in the form of God, thought it not robbery to be equal with God: But made himself of no reputation, and took upon him the form of a servant, and was made in the likeness of men: And being found in fashion as a man, he humbled himself, and became obedient unto death, even the death of the cross.

John 14:6

Jesus saith unto him, I am the way, the truth, and the life: no man cometh unto the Father, but by me.

Psalms 5:8

Lead me, O Lord, in thy righteousness because of mine enemies; make thy way straight before my face.

Psalms 91:2

John 6:63

It is the spirit that quickeneth; the flesh profiteth nothing: the words that I speak unto you, they are spirit, and they are life.

Hebrews 4:12

For the word of God is quick, and powerful, and sharper than any two-edged sword, piercing even to the dividing asunder of soul and spirit, and of the joints and marrow, and is a discerner of the thoughts and intents of the heart.

Isaiah 59:19

So shall they fear the name of the Lord from the west, and his glory from the rising of the sun. When the enemy shall come in like a flood, the Spirit of the Lord shall lift up a standard against him.

Exodus 14:14

The Lord shall fight for you, and ye shall hold your peace.

Psalms 91:3

John 8:31-32

Then said Jesus to those Jews which believed on him, If ye continue in my word, then are ye my disciples indeed; And ye shall know the truth, and the truth shall make you free.

Ephesians 1:4-6

According as he hath chosen us in him before the foundation of the world, that we should be holy and without blame before him in love: Having predestinated us unto the adoption of children by Jesus Christ to himself, according to the good pleasure of his will, To the praise of the glory of his grace, wherein he hath made us accepted in the beloved.

2 Corinthians 10:4-5

(For the weapons of our warfare are not carnal, but mighty through God to the pulling down of strong holds;) Casting down imaginations, and every high thing that exalteth itself against the knowledge of God, and bringing into captivity every thought to the obedience of Christ;

1 Corinthians 1:30

But of him are ye in Christ Jesus, who of God is made unto us wisdom, and righteousness, and sanctification, and redemption:

Psalms 91:4

Philippians 2:9-10

Wherefore God also hath highly exalted him, and given him a name which is above every name: That at the name of Jesus every knee should bow, of things in heaven, and things in earth, and things under the earth;

Matthew 28:18

And Jesus came and spake unto them, saying, All power is given unto me in heaven and in earth.

John 14:6

Jesus saith unto him, I am the way, the truth, and the life: no man cometh unto the Father, but by me.

John 16:33

These things I have spoken unto you, that in me ye might have peace. In the world ye shall have tribulation: but be of good cheer; I have overcome the world.

John 8:32

And ye shall know the truth, and the truth shall make you free.

Psalms 91:5

2 Timothy 1:7

For God hath not given us the spirit of fear; but of power, and of love, and of a sound mind.

Proverbs 3:5-6

Trust in the Lord with all thine heart; and lean not unto thine own understanding. In all thy ways acknowledge him, and he shall direct thy paths.

Proverbs 4:20-22

My son, attend to my words; incline thine ear unto my sayings. Let them not depart from thine eyes; keep them in the midst of thine heart. For they are life unto those that find them, and health to all their flesh.

James 4:7

Submit yourselves therefore to God. Resist the devil, and he will flee from you.

Psalms 62:2

He only is my rock and my salvation; he is my defence; I shall not be greatly moved

Psalms 91:6

2 Timothy 2:7

Consider what I say; and the Lord give thee understanding in all things.

James 1:2-5

My brethren, count it all joy when ye fall into divers temptations; Knowing this, that the trying of your faith worketh patience. But let patience have her perfect work, that ye may be perfect and entire, wanting nothing. If any of you lack wisdom, let him ask of God, that giveth to all men liberally, and upbraideth not; and it shall be given him.

Romans 8:28

And we know that all things work together for good to them that love God, to them who are the called according to his purpose.

Jeremiah 17:7-8

Blessed is the man that trusteth in the Lord, and whose hope the Lord is. For he shall be as a tree planted by the waters, and that spreadeth out her roots by the river, and shall not see when heat cometh, but her leaf shall be green;

and shall not be careful in the year of drought, neither shall cease from yielding fruit.

Psalms 91:7

Psalms 23:4

Yea, though I walk through the valley of the shadow of death, I will fear no evil: for thou art with me; thy rod and thy staff they comfort me.

Isaiah 54:17

No weapon that is formed against thee shall prosper; and every tongue that shall rise against thee in judgment thou shalt condemn. This is the heritage of the servants of the Lord, and their righteousness is of me, saith the Lord.

Revelation 12:11

And they overcame him by the blood of the Lamb, and by the word of their testimony; and they loved not their lives unto the death.

Psalms 91:8

Hebrews 11:6

But without faith it is impossible to please him: for he that cometh to God must believe that he is, and that he is a rewarder of them that diligently seek him.

Romans 14:23

And he that doubteth is damned if he eat, because he eateth not of faith: for whatsoever is not of faith is sin.

Ephesians 2:8

For by grace are ye saved through faith; and that not of yourselves: it is the gift of God:

Romans 4:3

For what saith the scripture? Abraham believed God, and it was counted unto him for righteousness.

2 Corinthians 5:21

For he hath made him to be sin for us, who knew no sin; that we might be made the righteousness of God in him.

Psalms 91:9

Romans 10:9

That if thou shalt confess with thy mouth the Lord Jesus, and shalt believe in thine heart that God hath raised him from the dead, thou shalt be saved.

John 10:30

I and my Father are one.

John 15:10

If ye keep my commandments, ye shall abide in my love; even as I have kept my Father's commandments, and abide in his love.

Psalms 91:10

Colossians 1:12

Giving thanks unto the Father, which hath made us meet to be partakers of the inheritance of the saints in light: Who hath delivered us from the power of darkness, and hath translated us into the kingdom of his dear Son:

Psalms 4:8

I will both lay me down in peace, and sleep: for thou, Lord, only makest me dwell in safety.

John 15:5

I am the vine, ye are the branches: He that abideth in me, and I in him, the same bringeth forth much fruit: for without me ye can do nothing.

Galatians 5:22-23

But the fruit of the Spirit is love, joy, peace, longsuffering, gentleness, goodness, faith, meekness, temperance: against such there is no law.

Psalms 91:11

Hebrews 1:14

Are they not all ministering spirits, sent forth to minister for them who shall be heirs of salvation?

Daniel 6:22

My God hath sent his angel, and hath shut the lions' mouths, that they have not hurt me:

Psalms 34:7

The angel of the Lord encampeth round about them that fear him, and delivereth them.

Psalms 103:20

Bless the Lord, ye his angels, that excel in strength, that do his commandments, hearkening unto the voice of his word.

Psalms 91:12

Hebrews 1:14

Are they not all ministering spirits, sent forth to minister for them who shall be heirs of salvation?

Psalms 119:105

Thy word is a lamp unto my feet, and a light unto my path.

Joshua 1:8

This book of the law shall not depart out of thy mouth; but thou shalt meditate therein day and night, that thou mayest observe to do according to all that is written therein: for then thou shalt make thy way prosperous, and then thou shalt have good success.

1 Corinthians 15:57

But thanks be to God, which giveth us the victory through our Lord Jesus Christ.

Psalms 91:13

James 1:14-15
But every man is tempted, when he is drawn away of his own lust, and enticed. Then when lust hath conceived, it bringeth forth sin: and sin, when it is finished, bringeth forth death.

1 Corinthians 10:13
There hath no temptation taken you but such as is common to man: but God is faithful, who will not suffer you to be tempted above that ye are able; but will with the temptation also make a way to escape, that ye may be able to bear it.

Luke 10:19
Behold, I give unto you power to tread on serpents and scorpions, and over all the power of the enemy: and nothing shall by any means hurt you.

Mark 16:18
They shall take up serpents; and if they drink any deadly thing, it shall not hurt them; they shall lay hands on the sick, and they shall recover.

Psalms 91:14

John 8:31-32

Then said Jesus to those Jews which believed on him, If ye continue in my word, then are ye my disciples indeed; And ye shall know the truth, and the truth shall make you free.

Colossians 3:2

Set your affection on things above, not on things on the earth.

Jeremiah 29:11

For I know the thoughts that I think toward you, saith the Lord, thoughts of peace, and not of evil, to give you an expected end.

Ephesians 1:4-5

According as he hath chosen us in him before the foundation of the world, that we should be holy and without blame before him in love: Having predestinated us unto the adoption of children by Jesus Christ to himself, according to the good pleasure of his will,

Ephesians 2:6

And hath raised us up together, and made us sit together in heavenly places in Christ Jesus:

Psalms 91:15

Mathew 6:33

But seek ye first the kingdom of God, and his righteousness; and all these things shall be added unto you.

Psalms 107:20

He sent his word, and healed them, and delivered them from their destructions.

1 Peter 5:6-7

Humble yourselves therefore under the mighty hand of God, that he may exalt you in due time: Casting all your care upon him; for he careth for you.

1 Samuel 2:30

Wherefore the Lord God of Israel saith, I said indeed that thy house, and the house of thy father, should walk before me for ever: but now the Lord saith, Be it far from me; for them that honour me I will honour, and they that despise me shall be lightly esteemed.

Psalms 91:16

John 3:16

For God so loved the world, that he gave his only begotten Son, that whosoever believeth in him should not perish, but have everlasting life.

Romans 5:1

Therefore being justified by faith, we have peace with God through our Lord Jesus Christ:

John 5:20

For the Father loveth the Son, and sheweth him all things that himself doeth: and he will shew him greater works than these, that ye may marvel.

Thank you for joining me on this journey, please let me know how this book transformed your prayer life by leaving me a book review on Amazon.

www.ingramcontent.com/pod-product-compliance
Lightning Source LLC
LaVergne TN
LVHW051510070426
835507LV00022B/3036